English Practice Year 1

Question Book

Emma Scott

Name _____

Schofield & Sims

Introduction

The **Schofield & Sims English Practice Year 1 Question Book** uses step-by-step practice to develop children's understanding of key English concepts. It covers every Year 1 objective in the 2014 National Curriculum programme of study.

The structure
This book is split into units, which are based on the key areas of the English curriculum for Year 1. These are:

- Grammar
- Punctuation
- Spelling
- Vocabulary
- Reading skills
- Read and respond.

Each double-page spread follows a consistent 'Practise', 'Extend' and 'Apply' sequence designed to deepen and reinforce learning. Each objective also includes a 'Remember' box that reminds children of the key information needed to help answer the questions.

There are three 'Read and respond' units in this book. Each 'Read and respond' unit is linked by an overarching theme and there is one fiction, one non-fiction and one poetry unit. Each text is accompanied by a set of comprehension questions, which practise reading skills such as inference, retrieval, summarising, prediction and analysis of word choice.

Additionally, a 'Writing skills' section allows children to apply the skills they have developed throughout the book in an extended writing task. The writing task is inspired by the themes covered in the 'Read and respond' units and gives opportunities for children to showcase their creative writing.

At the back of the book, there is a 'Final practice' section. Here, mixed questions are used to check children's understanding of the knowledge and skills acquired throughout the book and identify any areas that need to be revisited.

A mastery approach
The **Primary Practice English** series follows a knowledge-based mastery approach. The books have a focus on learning with purpose, to improve children's ability across all areas of English and to link learning in grammar, punctuation, spelling, vocabulary, reading and writing. There is frequent, varied practice and application of concepts to improve children's confidence when using their skills. A strong emphasis is given to vocabulary enrichment, reading for pleasure and reading stamina.

Assessment and checking progress
A 'Final practice' section is provided at the end of this book to check progress against the Year 1 English objectives. Children are given a target time of 45 minutes to complete this section, which is marked out of 20. Once complete, it enables them to assess their new knowledge and skills independently and to see the areas where they might need more practice.

Online answers
Answers for every question in this book are available to download from the **Schofield & Sims** website. The answers are accompanied by detailed explanations where helpful. There is also a progress chart, allowing children to track their learning as they complete each set of questions, and an editable certificate.

Contents

Unit 1: Grammar 4
Nouns and plural nouns 4
Making sentences 6
Joining words and sentences 8
Sequencing sentences 10

Unit 2: Punctuation 12
Capital letters for names and 'I' 12
Capital letters and full stops 14
Separating words 16
Question marks 18
Exclamation marks 20

Unit 3: Spelling 22
Letters and sounds 22
More letters and sounds 24
The /sh/, /ch/ and /th/ sounds 26
'ch' and 'tch' 28
'wh' and 'ph' 30
Hard and soft 'c' 32
Words ending 'ff', 'ss', 'zz', 'll' and 'ck' 34
Words with split digraphs 36
Adding the suffixes –ing and –ed 38
Adding the suffixes –er and –est 40
Adding the prefix un– 42
Words ending in 'y' 44

Unit 4: Vocabulary 46
Compound words 46
Days and numbers 48
Tricky words 50

Unit 5: Reading skills 52
Finding information 52
Ordering information 54
Thinking about words 56
Finding meaning 58

Unit 6: Read and respond: Stories 60
Peace at Last, by Jill Murphy 60
The Bear and the Piano, by David Litchfield 64

Unit 7: Read and respond: Information texts 68
How are stars made? 68
Your Heart and Lungs, by Sally Hewitt 72

Unit 8: Read and respond: Poems 76
Silver, by Walter de la Mare 76
Say How You Feel, by Joseph Coelho 78

Writing skills: What can you see at night? 82

Final practice 84

Nouns and plural nouns

Remember

A noun is a naming word. A singular noun names one thing: 'bird'. A plural noun names more than one thing: 'birds'. Add –s to change a singular noun into a plural noun. For example: 'bird' becomes 'bird**s**'. If a noun ends in 'sh', 'ch', 'ss', 's', 'x' or 'zz', add –es. For example: 'brush' becomes 'brush**es**'.

Practise

 1) Draw lines to match each singular noun to the correct plural noun.

box	pencils
pencil	socks
sock	glasses
glass	boxes

Extend

 2) Write the words in the correct box to show if they are singular nouns or plural nouns.

dog   classes   class   dogs   sweets   sweet

Singular nouns

Plural nouns

3 Write each of these nouns as a plural noun. One has been done for you.

a. apple   <u>_apples_</u>

b. ticket   _____

c. bus   _____

d. cup   _____

Apply

4 Rewrite the word given in brackets to make it a plural noun.

a. I picked some _____ (flower) for Mum.

b. We had _____ (pancake) for dinner.

c. We washed the _____ (dish) together.

d. There was lots of litter in the _____ (bush) next to the road.

e. My brother and I both got new _____ (watch) for our birthdays.

Making sentences

> **Remember**
>
> A sentence is a group of words that starts with a capital letter and ends with a full stop, for example: '**N**adiya likes eating ice cream**.**' The words must be in the correct order and must make sense. Always leave a space between each word when writing a sentence.

Practise

1 Tick to show if the sentence makes sense.

Betsy tired ☐   Betsy is tired. ☐

hot today ☐   It is hot today. ☐

Reading is fun. ☐   books is ☐

Extend

2 Write the words in the correct order to make a sentence. One has been done for you.

a. teacher   My   kind.   is

My teacher is kind.

b. I   cakes.   love   baking

_____

c. kitten   The   is   cute.

_____

d. my   ride   I   scooter.

_____

3 Write the correct word from the box to complete each sentence.

> She   My   bike   bank   reading   I

a. _____ like eating pizza.

b. I enjoy riding my _____.

c. We love _____ books.

d. _____ team won the match.

e. _____ is strong.

f. Sasha works in a _____.

Apply

4 Write a sentence about each picture.

a.

_____
_____
_____

b.

_____
_____
_____

Tip Say your sentence aloud before you write it. Then you can make sure that it makes sense.

Joining words and sentences

Remember

The word 'and' is a joining word. Use 'and' to join words together. For example: 'fish **and** chips'. The word 'and' can also be used to join two sentences together. For example, the sentences 'I like running. I like jumping.' can be joined to make 'I like running **and** I like jumping.'

 **Practise**

1) Write 'and' to join these words together.

   a. pens _____ pencils

   b. toast _____ jam

   c. night _____ day

   d. socks _____ shoes

2) Join each pair of sentences to make **one** new sentence using 'and'.

   a. I like reading. I like watching films.

   _____

   b. I have a bike. I have a scooter.

   _____

   c. She loves jelly. She loves ice cream.

   _____

   d. He plays the piano. He plays the drums.

   _____

Extend

3 Complete these sentences using 'and'. One has been done for you.

a.  I went to the shop to buy <u>bread and jam</u>.

b.  I went to the shop to buy _____.

c.  I went to the shop to buy _____.

d. 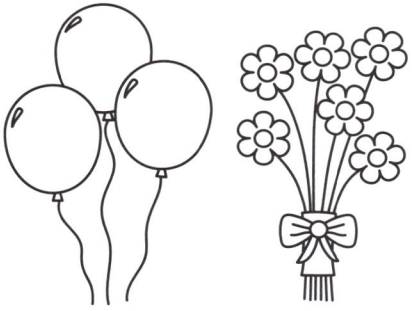 I went to the shop to buy _____.

Apply

4 Complete these sentences using your own ideas.

a. I went to the zoo and _____.

b. Jack fell over and _____.

c. I go to school and _____.

d. Jan went to the park and _____.

Sequencing sentences

Remember

Sentences can be joined together to make a piece of writing. This writing could be a story or information about something. The sentences should be in the correct order or sequence so that the writing makes sense.

Practise

1. Tick to show if the sentences are in the correct order.

a. I planted a seed. I gave the seed some water. The seed grew into a plant. ☐

b. I ate the sandwich. I put cheese on the bread. I spread butter on the bread. ☐

c. Toby took out his phone. He pressed the buttons to call Lola. He spoke to Lola. ☐

d. Mum read her book. Mum opened her book. Mum chose a book from the shelf. ☐

Tip Some things need to happen before other things. Read the sentences and think about what you would need to do first.

Extend

2. Write 1, 2 or 3 to put the sentences in the correct order.

The big bad wolf tried to blow the house down. _____

The three little pigs decided to build a house. _____

The first little pig built a house made of straw. _____

3 Underline the sentence that best follows the first two sentences.

a. Layla squeezed toothpaste on to her toothbrush. She turned on the tap.

She brushed her teeth.   She ate her toast.   She plaited her hair.

b. Romesh put on his shoes. He tied his shoelaces.

He fell asleep.   He found a secret cave.   He left the house.

c. Goldilocks went into the house. She saw three bowls of porridge.

She ran up the hill.   She put it in her bag.   She ate the porridge.

Apply

4 Write **two** sentences to show what is happening in the pictures. You could use some of the words in the box to help you.

children   gift   party   games

a. _____

_____

b. _____

_____

Capital letters for names and 'I'

Remember

Always use a capital letter when writing someone's name, for example: '**A**nna'. Place names, days of the week and months also start with a capital letter: '**R**ome', '**M**onday', '**J**uly'. You should use a capital letter when you write about yourself and use the word 'I'.

Practise

1. Underline all of the capital letters in the sentences below.

    a. Ahmed loves playing on his computer.

    b. My sister is called Nicola and her birthday is in January.

    c. I went to a party on Sunday.

    d. Mr Green is my favourite teacher at Sunnyside School.

Extend

2. Tick to show if the word should start with a capital letter.

    a.  paris ☐

    b.  sandwich ☐

    c.  koala ☐

    d.  cinderella ☐

③ Complete each name or month using a capital letter. The first letter is given in brackets.

a. _____luffy (f)

b. _____ctober (o)

c. _____dward (e)

d. _____olly (p)

Apply

④ Write **two** sentences about yourself starting with the word 'I'. You could write about where you live, a place you have visited, who your best friend is or what your pet is called. For example:

I live in a town in Scotland. I have a pet hamster called Nibbles.

_____

_____.

_____

_____.

Primary Practice **English Year 1**

Capital letters and full stops

> **Remember**
>
> A sentence always starts with a capital letter and usually ends with a full stop. For example: '**W**e went swimming**.**'

Practise

1) Tick the sentences that start with a capital letter and end with a full stop.

We went to the farm. ☐

i need to sit down ☐

It rained all day. ☐

the leaves fell from the tree ☐

i have a packed lunch today ☐

My dad read the newspaper. ☐

2) Rewrite the incorrect sentences from **Question 1** so that they start with a capital letter and end with a full stop.

_____

_____

_____

_____

Extend

3 Underline the letters that should be capital letters and write the missing full stops in these sentences.

  a. fatima played on the swings ___

  b. the crab hid under the rock ___

  c. we ate pizza for dinner ___

  d. i love playing in the sandpit ___

4 Choose **one** sentence from **Question 3** and rewrite it, adding the capital letter and the full stop.

_____

Apply

5 Write **two** sentences about this picture. Remember to use capital letters and full stops.

_____

_____

_____

Primary Practice **English Year 1**

Separating words

Remember

Each word in a sentence should be separated so that it makes sense to the person reading it. For example: 'Owlshuntatnight' should be separated as 'Owls hunt at night'. Each word should be separated by a space.

Practise

1. Tick the sentences that use spaces correctly.

   a. Myteddyissoft. ☐   My teddy is soft. ☐

   b. I ran to catch the bus. ☐   Irantocatchthebus. ☐

   c. Tom scored a goal. ☐   Tomscoredagoal. ☐

   d. Giraffesaretall. ☐   Giraffes are tall. ☐

Extend

2. Circle the **two** words that should have a space between them in each of these sentences.

   a. Wewent for a long walk.

   b. The stars werebright.

   c. Mum reada book.

   d. Dadcooked us breakfast.

Tip You could read each sentence aloud to see where the space should go. There should be one at the end of each word.

3 Rewrite these sentences using spaces to separate the words.

a. Ilovepopcorn.

_____

b. Thepuppyiscute.

_____

Apply

4 Write a sentence about each picture. Remember to use spaces to separate the words.

a.

b.

a. _____

_____

b. _____

_____

Question marks

Remember

Some sentences are questions. A question is a sentence that asks something and has an answer. Use a question mark to end a sentence that is a question. For example: 'What did you eat for lunch today**?**'

Practise

1) Copy the question marks.

? ___ ___ ___ ___ ___ ___

2) Read the sentences and write a question mark at the end of each one.

a. Who is coming to the party ___

b. How many goals did the football team score ___

c. Which toy should I buy ___

d. Where are you going on holiday this year ___

Tip A question mark always goes at the end of a sentence.

3) Tick the sentences that should end with a question mark.

Will it rain later ☐   Pop the balloon ☐

When does the show start ☐   She won a medal ☐

Unit 2 • Punctuation

Extend

4 Draw lines to match each question to its answer.

Where are you going?	I am eating a sandwich.
How are you?	I am going to the park.
When are you leaving?	I am well.
What are you eating?	I am leaving this morning.

Apply

5 Write the words in the correct order to make question sentences. Remember to add the question mark in the correct place.

a. animals   at   we   What   zoo   will   the   see

_____

b. we   to   go   swimming   the   Can   pool

_____

c. the   Will   shop   open   be   gift

_____

d. is   the   stop   Where   nearest   bus

_____

Tip Remember that a question usually starts with a question word, such as 'who' or 'what'.

Primary Practice **English Year 1**

19

Exclamation marks

Remember

Some sentences end with an exclamation mark. The exclamation mark shows there are strong feelings like anger, shock or surprise. For example: 'I am very cross with you**!**', 'I cannot believe it**!**' Exclamation marks can also show that someone is speaking loudly or shouting: 'Watch out for the car**!**'

Practise

1) Copy the exclamation marks.

   !

   ___   ___   ___   ___   ___   ___

2) Read the sentences and write an exclamation mark at the end of each one.

   a. That game was amazing ___

   b. Leave me alone ___

   c. I am so pleased to finally meet you ___

   d. She just broke the world record ___

3) Tick the sentences that should end with an exclamation mark.

   Bang ☐   How does this work ☐

   What a lovely day ☐   What time is the next bus ☐

Tip Exclamation marks go at the end of sentences that show loud noises or strong feelings.

Extend

4 Complete each sentence so that it ends with an exclamation mark.

a.  Keep off _____

b.  Stop _____

Apply

5 Write a sentence about each picture. Use an exclamation mark for each one.

a.  b.

a. _____

_____

b. _____

_____

Letters and sounds

> **Remember**
>
> These questions practise some of the letters and sounds that may be familiar from Reception. Break words into sounds to spell them by writing the grapheme for each sound. For example: 'dog' can be broken down as 'd-o-g' and 'sock' can be broken down as 's-o-ck'.

Practise

1) Write the correct word under each picture.

a.

b.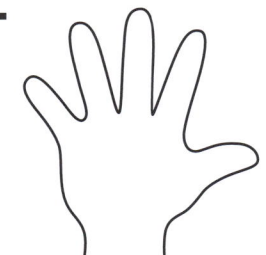

c.

_____

_____

_____

d.

e.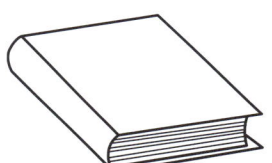

f.

_____

_____

_____

2) Write the correct letter to complete each word.

a.  | w | | b |

b.  | | i | n |

 **Extend**

3 Write 'a', 'e', 'i', 'o' or 'u' to complete each word.

a.  f___x   b.  t___n

c.  c___t   d.  j___g

4 Change the bold letter in the first word to make two new words. One has been done for you.

a. s**u**n   _f_un   _b_un

b. ma**t**   ma___   ma___

c. **b**in   ___in   ___in

d. ra**n**   ra___   ra___

 **Apply**

5 Tick the sentences that are true for you.

I have long hair. ☐   I have a pet dog. ☐

I have a sister. ☐   I have short hair. ☐

I am a boy. ☐   I like painting. ☐

More letters and sounds

> **Remember**
>
> Two letters that go together to make one sound are called a digraph. For example: 'ai' in 'r**ai**n' and 'ng' in 'ri**ng**'. Some sounds can be written in more than one way. For example, the /oi/ sound can be written as 'oi' (as in 's**oi**l') or 'oy' (as in 'b**oy**').

Practise

1   **a.** Circle the things that have the /oi/ sound in them.

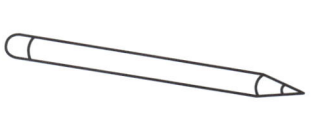   

    b. Circle the things that have the /ee/ sound in them.

 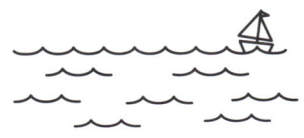  

2   Draw lines to match each digraph to the picture that has the digraph in it.

Extend

3 Write the correct letters from the box to complete each word.

a.    ____eep   sh   ch

b.    br____m    oo   ee

c.    si____   nk   ng

Apply

4 Complete this crossword using the clues. One has been done for you.

Across

2. You see it in the sky.
4. An animal that lives on a farm.

Down

1. You play with it.
3. An animal that is a pet.

The /sh/, /ch/ and /th/ sounds

Remember

When 'h' is added to 's', 'c' or 't', it changes the sound. 's' and 'h' together make the /sh/ sound, for example: '**sh**ip', 'ru**sh**'. 'c' and 'h' together make the /ch/ sound: '**ch**art', 'lun**ch**'. 't' and 'h' together make the /th/ sound: '**th**ree', 'fro**th**'.

Practise

1. Sort these words into the table. One has been done for you.

   chap   ~~shoot~~   this   much   mash   froth

/sh/ sound	/ch/ sound	/th/ sound
shoot		

2. Circle the word that matches the picture.

   a.    churn   church   chat   much

   b.   rush   shop   ship   brush

   c.   sloth   think   thing   slip

Extend

3 Write 'sh', 'ch' or 'th' to complete each word.

a.  ____ick

b. 3 ____ree

c.  ____ell

d.  tee____

4 Draw lines to match the letters to make a word.

 sh   ew

 ch   ing

 th   arp

Tip Try each /sh/, /ch/ and /th/ sound with each ending to see which one makes a real word. Make sure the word you have made is also spelt correctly.

Apply

5 Use the clue to find a word that begins or ends with 'sh', 'ch' or 'th'. The first letter has been given.

a. the opposite of thick   t_____

b. an animal that swims   f_____

c. a meal that you eat   l_____

d. something you sit on   c_____

e. somewhere you buy things   s_____

'ch' and 'tch'

Remember

Many words end with the /ch/ sound, such as 'lun**ch**'. However, the /ch/ sound can also be spelt 'tch'. For example: 'wa**tch**'. A /ch/ sound at the end of a word is usually made by the grapheme 'tch' rather than 'ch' if it comes immediately after a short vowel sound.

Practise

1) Sort these words into the table.

beach   patch   hutch   punch   witch
sketch   march   pitch   torch   catch

Words that end with 'ch'	Words that end with 'tch'

Extend

2) Now add at least two more words to each column in the table in **Question 1**.

Tip Remember to think about the rules for using 'ch' or 'tch' when spelling the words.

3 Tick to show if each word ends in 'ch' or 'tch'. Write the correct ending to complete each word.

a. ma_____   ch ☐   tch ☐

b. crun_____   ch ☐   tch ☐

c. ben_____   ch ☐   tch ☐

d. pi_____   ch ☐   tch ☐

Apply

4 Draw lines to match each sentence to the correct picture.

We throw a stick for our dog to fetch.

The caterpillar had a munch on the apple.

Dad told me to switch the light off.

Polly the parrot sat on her perch.

'wh' and 'ph'

> **Remember**
>
> The /f/ sound can be spelt 'f' or 'ph'. For example: '**f**rog', '**ph**onics'.
> The /w/ sound can be spelt 'w' or 'wh'. For example: '**w**alk', '**wh**isper'.

Practise

1. Write 'w' or 'wh' to spell the names of these animals.

   a.

   _____ale

   b.

   _____orm

Extend

2. Unscramble the letters to make the correct word.

   a.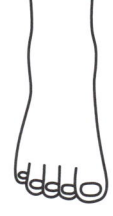

   ootf _____

   b.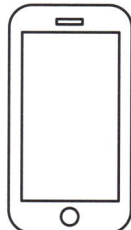

   oneph _____

   c.

   eewhl _____

   d.

   psaw _____

3 Circle the words in the box that have 'wh' or 'ph'. Complete the sentences using the words from the box.

> fork   alphabet   white   trophy   fire   wheat

a. There are 26 letters in the _____.

b. The farmer grew _____ in her field.

c. My team won the _____.

d. Our cat has a _____ tail.

Apply

4 Finish the pictures to match the sentences.

a. My shirt is white with birds on it.

b. My shirt is green with elephants on it.

c. My shirt is red with cats with long whiskers on it.

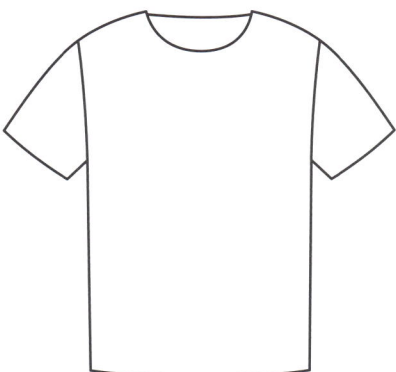

d. My shirt is blue with a dolphin on it.

Hard and soft 'c'

> **Remember**
>
> The letter 'c' makes the hard /c/ sound in words like '**c**at'. The hard /c/ sound can also be be made by the letter 'k' before 'e', 'i' and 'y' or by the letters 'ck'. For example: 'ca**k**e', '**k**ic**k**', 's**k**y'. When 'c' comes before 'e', 'i' or 'y', it makes a soft /s/ sound such as in 'mi**c**e', '**c**ircus' or '**c**ycle'.

Practise

1) Sort these words into the table depending on which sound the 'c' makes.

dice   can   city   crisps   catch   rice

Hard /c/ sound	Soft /s/ sound

2) Tick the words that have a hard /c/ sound.

mice ☐   fork ☐

dark ☐   space ☐

drink ☐   picnic ☐

ice ☐   prince ☐

Unit 3 • Spelling

Extend

3 Write the words that you ticked in **Question 2** to complete these sentences.

   a. I eat my dinner with a knife and _____.

   b. It is _____ outside at night.

   c. I was thirsty so I had a sip of my _____.

   d. We had a _____ at the park.

4 Write 'c' or 'k' to complete these words.

   a.    **b.** 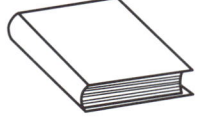   **c.**    **d.**

   ___up   boo___   ___andle   sin___

Apply

5 Read the text and underline all of the words where 'c' makes a soft /s/ sound. Circle the words that have the hard /c/ sound.

Kim had her birthday in December. She wanted a cat, but Mum did not like pets. Mum took her to Central Shopping Hall to choose a present. The roads were icy, and the car skidded, but Mum was a good driver. At the shops Kim saw a coat she liked, but when she went back it had gone. Kim picked a cuddly cat instead. She called it Crumpet.

Words ending 'ff', 'ss', 'zz', 'll' and 'ck'

Remember

Words ending in the sounds /f/, /s/, /z/ and /l/ can often be written with double letters at the end rather than a single letter. Words ending in the /k/ sound can often be spelt 'ck'. This usually happens if the /f/, /s/, /z/, /l/ or /k/ sound comes after a short vowel. For example: 'pu**ff**', 'cro**ss**', 'bu**zz**', 'fu**ll**', 'ti**ck**'.

Practise

1. Tick to show whether each word has the 'ff', 'ss', 'zz', 'll' or 'ck' spelling. One has been done for you.

	ff	ss	zz	ll	ck
off	✓				
kick					
fuss					
doll					
fizz					

Extend

2. Choose the correct letters from the box for each word. Write the letters to complete the word.

   a. ki_____   [ss   zz]   **b.** be_____   [ff   ll]

   c. du_____   [zz   ck]   **d.** stu_____   [ff   ll]

Unit 3 • Spelling

③ Draw lines to match each word beginning to the correct ending.

le		zz
fi		ss
so		ff
flu		ll
te		ck

Tip If a word beginning can go with two endings, leave it until the end and go back to it.

Apply

④ Write a sentence about each picture using the words in the box.

a.

| long dress doll frills |

_____
_____

b.

| rocket whizz zoom air |

_____
_____

Words with split digraphs

Remember

A split digraph is when one sound is written with two letters that are split in a word. The split digraphs are 'i-e' (/igh/) as in 't**i**m**e**' 'a-e' (/ai/) as in 'b**a**k**e**', 'o-e' (/oa/) as in 'st**o**n**e**', 'u-e' (/oo/ or /yoo/) as in 'fl**u**t**e**' or 't**u**b**e**' and 'e-e' (/ee/) as in 'th**e**s**e**'.

Practise

1) Draw lines to match each sentence to the correct picture.

I go on the slide.

I go inside.

I play with a kite.

I like to ride a bike.

 **Extend**

② Write the correct word under each picture. All of the words have a split digraph.

a.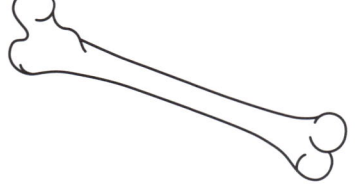

b.

c.

_____   _____   _____

 Apply

③ Look at the picture. Write **two** sentences about what you can see. Use the words in the box to help.

fire   smoke   kite   bike   cake   grapes

_____

_____

_____

Primary Practice **English Year 1**   37

Adding the suffixes –ing and –ed

Remember

Add the suffixes –ing and –ed to the end of some words to make a new word. For example: 'jump' + –ing becomes 'jump**ing**'; 'jump' + –ed becomes 'jump**ed**'. The spelling of 'jump' does not change when the suffix is added.

Practise

(1) Add –ing and –ed to the word 'hunt' to make two new words.

a. hunt + ing = _____

b. hunt + ed = _____

Extend

(2) Look at the pictures and write a word ending with –ing. The first letter of each word is given.

a.

j_____

b.

s_____

c.

l_____

Unit 3 • Spelling

③ Write what is happening in each picture using a word that ends with –ing. One has been done for you.

a.    Anna is __reading__.

b.    Sam is _____.

c.    Miss Green is _____.

d.    Amir is _____.

💭 Apply

④ Add –ing or –ed to the word given in brackets to make each sentence make sense.

a. Yesterday I _____ (push) my little sister on the swing.

b. My big brother is _____ (work) on his computer in his room.

Adding the suffixes –er and –est

Remember

Writers use words called adjectives to describe things, people or places. For example: 'the **small** mouse'.

The suffixes –er and –est can be added to describing words to change the meaning and make words that compare things. For example, adding the suffix –er to 'small' in 'small mouse' makes 'small**er** mouse'. Adding the suffix –est to 'small' in 'small mouse' makes 'small**est** mouse'.

Practise

1. Circle the word that makes sense in each sentence.

   a. The dog is **meaner** / **meanest** than the cat.

   b. He was the **prouder** / **proudest** dad in the room.

Extend

2. Look at the picture. Write the correct word 'taller' or 'shorter' to complete the sentences.

   a. The giraffe is _____ than the zebra.

   b. The zebra is _____ than the giraffe.

③ Look at the pictures. Write a word that ends with –er and a word that ends –est for each one. Two have been done for you.

a.

hot   _hotter_   _hottest_

b.

slow   _____   _____

c.    

small   _____   _____

Apply

④ Write a sentence about these objects. Include a describing word that ends with –er or –est.

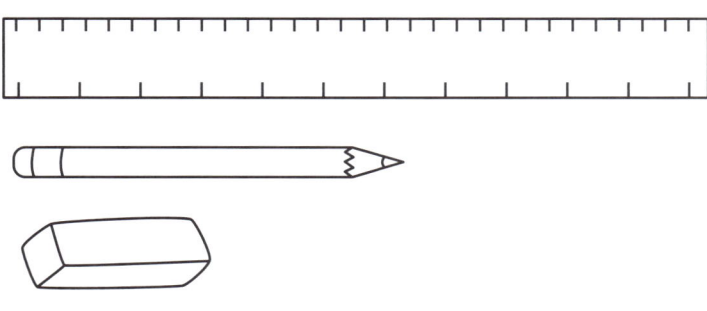

_____

_____

Primary Practice **English Year 1**   **41**

Adding the prefix un–

Remember

The prefix un– can be added to the beginning of some words to make them mean the opposite. For example: 'pack' becomes '**un**pack', 'zip' becomes '**un**zip'.

Practise

1 Write un– in front of these words to make new words that mean the opposite.

a. _____ fair   b. _____ kind

c. _____ load   d. _____ lock

e. _____ well   f. _____ able

2 Rewrite each word and add 'un' to the beginning to make it mean the opposite. One has been done for you.

a. fit _unfit_   b. dress _____

c. do _____   d. lucky _____

e. cover _____   f. wanted _____

Extend

3 Write a word beginning with un– that means the same as the word in bold.

a. **sad** _____   b. **messy** _____

c. **dangerous** _____ d. **false** _____

e. **ill** _____   f. **brave** _____

4 Find the **six** un– words from **Question 3** in the word search. The words run horizontally and vertically.

U	N	T	R	U	E	U	R	A
N	F	I	H	B	F	N	J	U
T	Y	D	U	K	N	A	F	N
I	Z	X	N	P	H	F	S	H
D	Y	U	W	I	U	R	D	A
Y	O	O	E	I	T	A	T	P
O	T	W	L	C	H	I	X	P
X	I	P	L	A	I	D	Z	Y
N	U	N	S	A	F	E	L	P

Apply

5 Write **four** sentences using **four** of the un– words from the word search in **Question 4**.

a. _____

_____

b. _____

_____

c. _____

_____

d. _____

_____

Words ending in 'y'

> **Remember**
>
> Sometimes at the end of words, the /ee/ sound is spelt 'y'. For example: 'funn**y**', 'happ**y**'.

Practise

1 **a.** Sort these words into the table depending on which sound the 'y' makes.

> yell   very   yellow   lady   carry   yak

/ee/ as in 'happy'	/y/ as in 'yes'

b. What do you notice about all the words in the first column? Add another word to each column.

_____

2 Circle the words in the cloud that end with the /ee/ sound spelt 'y'.

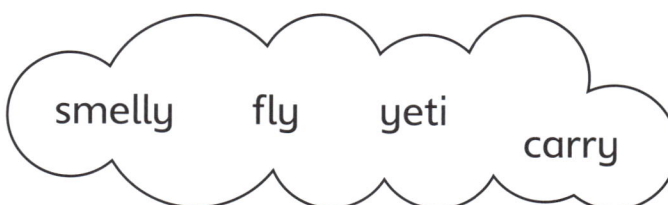

smelly   fly   yeti   carry

Unit 3 • Spelling

Extend

3 Write the word from the box to match the picture.

> baby   sunny   jelly   funny

a.

_____

b.

_____

c.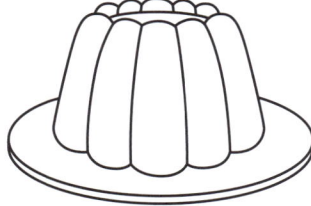

_____

d.

_____

Apply

4 Read this text. Circle the /ee/ sounds spelt 'y'. Put a box around the /ee/ sounds spelt 'ee'. Underline any other /ee/ sounds.

Sally went to the beach. It was so sunny that Sally felt happy and cheerful all day. She played in the sand and put seaweed in her bucket to collect crabs. The crabs felt tickly walking on her hand. At the end of the day she got a peach ice cream.

Tip Read the text aloud and listen to the sounds.

Compound words

> **Remember**
>
> A compound word is a word made up of two words. For example: the words 'bed' and 'room' together make the compound word 'bedroom'; 'lady' and 'bird' make the compound word 'ladybird'.

Practise

1 Write compound words using the picture clues.

a.   p _ _ c _ _ _

b. 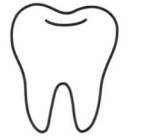 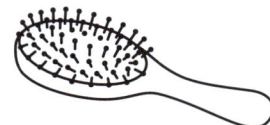 t _ _ _ _ b _ _ _ _

c.  h _ _ _ b _ _

Extend

2 Draw lines to join the words to make compound words.

rain	flower
sun	bow
rail	fly
butter	way

Unit 4 • Vocabulary

Schofield & Sims

③ Write the **four** compound words you found in **Question 2**.

_____   _____

_____   _____

💭 Apply

④ Write **three** words from the box that go with 'ball' to make new compound words.

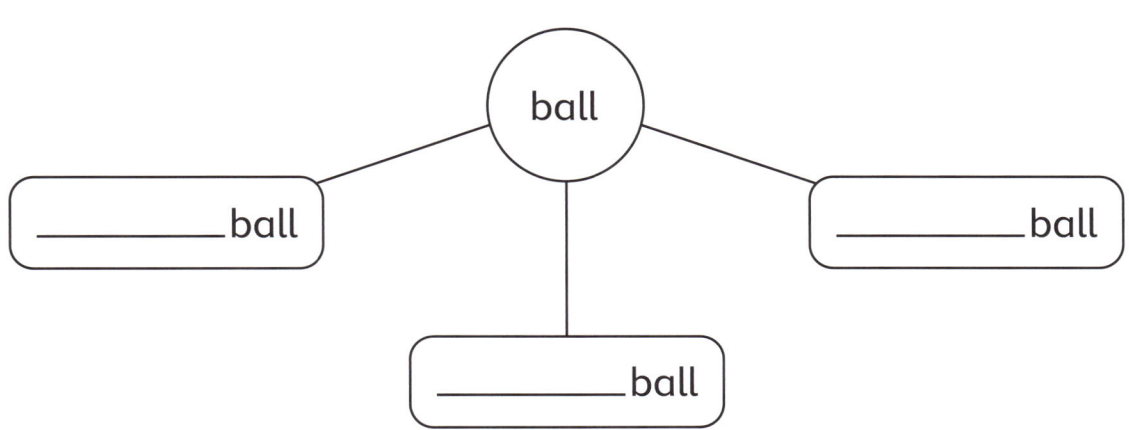

⑤ Write **three** sentences using **one** of the compound words you made in **Question 4** in each sentence.

a. _____

_____

b. _____

_____

c. _____

_____

Days and numbers

Remember

It is important to spell common words, such as days of the week and numbers, correctly. Days of the week always start with a capital letter, for example: '**M**onday'. Numbers can be written as digits or words: 1 can be written 'one'; 16 can be written 'sixteen'.

Practise

(1) Use the days of the week in the box to answer these questions.

> Saturday   Monday   Sunday   Wednesday

a. What is the first day of the week? _____

b. Which day of the week has nine letters? _____

c. Which two days are the weekend?

_____ and _____

Extend

(2) Draw lines to match each number to the correct spelling.

2	nine
8	five
9	eight
5	two

Unit 4 • Vocabulary

3) Write each number as a word.

a. 10 _____   b. 7 _____

c. 20 _____   d. 15 _____

Apply

4) Complete these sentences in your own words. Remember to write any numbers as words.

a. I am _____ years old.

b. My favourite day of the week is _____

because _____

_____.

5) Unscramble the number words. Write the correct spelling of each word on the line.

a. etn _____

b. eon _____

c. eensnteven _____

6) Unscramble these words to make days of the week. Write the correct spelling of each word on the line.

a. Tsdayue _____

b. dayThrsu _____

c. ydFira _____

d. onMayd _____

Tricky words

> **Remember**
>
> There are some words that cannot be sounded out and must be learnt, for example: 'the', 'said', 'was'. These are called tricky words. The letters or groups of letters in these words do not make the sounds they usually make.

Practise

 1) Find these words in the word search. The words run horizontally and vertically.

| our | once | house | today | come |

I	A	K	D	K	H	O	U	S	E
B	N	C	L	I	X	Z	I	T	S
Q	U	O	J	A	X	O	S	J	W
U	Y	M	O	Q	F	I	Q	V	R
I	Z	E	L	I	O	G	H	I	O
U	T	W	F	J	O	X	W	O	Z
T	H	T	O	D	A	Y	F	U	Q
Z	A	O	N	C	E	R	T	R	G
O	I	U	G	H	C	R	N	N	C
Q	O	E	S	B	V	X	K	S	P

50 Unit 4 • *Vocabulary* Schofield & Sims

Extend

2) Write the correct word from the box to complete each sentence.

> where   ask   by   some

a. I would like _____ salt on my chips.

b. Samir put his hand up to _____ a question.

c. _____ are you going?

d. We live _____ the sea.

3) Unscramble these words to make one of the tricky words from the box. Write the correct spelling of the word on the line.

> school   said   was   love

a. dais _____   **b.** velo _____

c. choosl _____   **d.** swa _____

Apply

4) Write **two** sentences using **one** word from the box in each sentence.

> were   here   where   there

a. _____

_____

b. _____

_____

Primary Practice **English Year 1**   **51**

Finding information

Remember

To answer questions about a text, read the words carefully. Pictures can also be useful for finding out information about a text. There are different types of texts, such as stories (called fiction), information texts (called non-fiction) and poetry.

Practise

 1) Draw lines to match the pictures to the correct sentences.

The fish swims in the bowl.

Miles and Anika cross the road.

Tom plays a game on his computer.

The family are camping.

52   Unit 5 • Reading skills   Schofield & Sims

Extend

2 Here is some information about elephants. Read the information carefully, then circle the correct words in the sentences below.

> There are three species of elephant in the world. Elephants eat plants, such as leaves and grasses. Did you know that elephants travel together in a group called a herd?

a. There are **two / three** different species of elephant.

b. Elephants eat **meat / plants**.

c. Elephants travel **on their own / in a group**.

Apply

3 Read this short story and answer the questions below.

> Hansel and Gretel went out into the woods. It was very dark and they got lost. They found a house made of sweets and gingerbread. A witch lived in the house. She trapped them but they escaped.

a. Why did the children get lost?

_____

b. What was the house they found made of? Write **two** things.

_____ and _____

c. Did the children escape? Tick **one**.   Yes ☐   No ☐

Primary Practice **English Year 1**   53

Ordering information

Remember

Sometimes it can be useful to order things that happen in a story or information in a non-fiction text. To do this, read the text carefully and remember what happened and when. It is a good idea to read the text more than once to help check and order events.

Practise

 1 Look at the pictures. Write 1, 2 or 3 to put the words in the correct order.

a.

eat _____

mix _____

cook _____

b.

grow _____

plant _____

dig _____

c.

launch _____

land _____

zoom _____

 **Extend**

2 Write 1, 2 or 3 to put the sentences in the story in the correct order.

They found the chest of gold.   The pirates found a treasure map.   They sailed on their ship.

_____   _____   _____

3 Read these sentences carefully. Write 1, 2, 3 or 4 to put the sentences in the correct order.

Ben puts on a stamp.   _____

Ben writes the letter.   _____

Amy gets the letter in the post.   _____

Ben posts the letter.   _____

 **Apply**

4 Read the sentences carefully. Write the final sentence to create a familiar story.

Jack was a boy who lived with his mum.

He sold their cow for a magic bean.

He planted the bean and it grew and grew.

_____

Primary Practice **English Year 1**

Thinking about words

> **Remember**
>
> Different words can have the same meaning. For example, in the sentences 'The man was **angry** when the car splashed him' and 'The man was **furious** when the car splashed him', the words 'angry' and 'furious' mean the same thing.

Practise

 1 Circle the word that is the odd one out in each set. It has a different meaning to the other two words.

- **a.** sad   miserable   scared
- **b.** small   huge   gigantic
- **c.** quiet   noisy   loud
- **d.** fast   speedy   bad

Extend

 2 Draw lines to match the words that have the same meaning. One has been done for you.

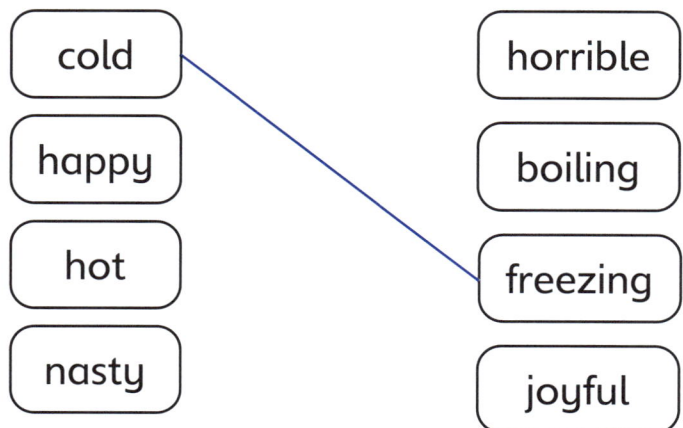

3 Read each of these sentences. Look carefully at the underlined word. Circle the word in the box with the same meaning.

a. Under the bridge lived a hideous troll. | nice   beautiful   ugly

b. I found the maths homework simple. | easy   difficult   silly

c. We were tired after the long journey. | busy   sleepy   ready

Apply

4 Read the text and answer the questions.

> At the weekend, Joshua went to the fairground. He was very excited. First, he went for a ride on the roller coaster, which twisted speedily along the rails. After he had been on some rides, he decided to gobble up some sweet and sticky candyfloss. He had a brilliant day.

a. Find and copy **one** word that means the same as 'turned'.

_____

b. Find and copy **one** word that tells you that the roller coaster moved quickly.

_____

c. What do the words 'gobble up' mean? Tick **one**.

play ☐   eat ☐   sleep ☐

Finding meaning

Remember

There are often clues in a text to help you understand why something happened or how a character feels. For example: 'Ella stamped her foot when Mum asked her to get ready for school.' The words 'stamped her foot' show that Ella does not want to get ready for school.

Practise

1) Write the correct word from the box under each picture.

tired   happy   sad

a.

b.

c.

_____   _____   _____

Extend

2) Read the sentence. Look for clues that tell you what has happened. Tick the correct answer.

Ayra kicked the ball. The crowd cheered.

Ayra missed a goal. ☐   Ayra scored a goal. ☐

Tip Imagine watching someone kick a ball. When would you cheer?

3 Read the sentences. Underline the word or group of words that give a clue about how the character is feeling. Write how you think the character is feeling.

   a. The sun was shining. Chloe grinned as she put on her sandals. She opened the door.

   Chloe was feeling _____.

   b. George found the cave. He could hear the dragon roaring. He tiptoed inside.

   George was feeling _____.

Apply

4 Read the text below and answer the questions.

> The big day had finally arrived. Shona got out of bed, jumped up and down and went downstairs. It was silent. Where was everybody? Her heart sank. Usually, her family were there to wish her happy birthday. She opened the kitchen door. "Surprise!" shouted the voices coming from inside.
> A large grin crept across Shona's face. Her family hadn't forgotten about her birthday after all.

   a. What was 'the big day'? _____

   b. How was Shona feeling when she first went downstairs?

   _____

   c. Which words tell you this? _____

   d. Who shouted "Surprise!"? _____

Peace at Last, by Jill Murphy

> *Peace at Last* is a picture book written and illustrated by the well-loved children's author Jill Murphy. Mr Bear and his family go to bed, but Mr Bear cannot get to sleep because of Mrs Bear's snoring. He tries to sleep in lots of different places, but he just cannot seem to find any peace and quiet.

TICK-TOCK … went the living room clock … TICK-TOCK, TICK-TOCK. CUCKOO! CUCKOO!

"Oh NO!" said Mr Bear, "I can't stand THIS!"

So he went off to sleep in the kitchen.

DRIP, DRIP … went the leaky kitchen tap. HMMMMMMMMMM … went the refrigerator.

"Oh NO," said Mr Bear, "I can't stand THIS."

So he got up and went to sleep in the garden.

Well, you would not believe what noises there are in the garden at night.

"TOO-WHIT-TOO-WHOO!" went the owl.

"SNUFFLE, SNUFFLE," went the hedgehog.

"MIAAAOW!" sang the cats on the wall.

"Oh NO!" said Mr Bear, "I can't stand THIS."

So he went off to sleep in the car.

It was cold in the car and uncomfortable, but Mr Bear was so tired that he didn't notice.

He was just falling asleep when all the birds started to sing and the sun peeped in at the window.

"TWEET TWEET!" went the birds. SHINE, SHINE … went the sun.

"Oh NO!" said Mr Bear, "I can't stand THIS."

So he got up and went back into the house.

In the house, Baby Bear was fast asleep, and Mrs Bear had turned over and wasn't snoring any more. Mr Bear got into bed and closed his eyes.

"Peace at last," he said to himself.

BRRRRRRRRRRRRRRR! went the alarm clock, BRRRRRR!

Mrs Bear sat up and rubbed her eyes.

"Good morning, dear," she said.

"Did you sleep well?"

"Not VERY well, dear," yawned Mr Bear.

Peace at Last, by Jill Murphy

1) Where does Mr Bear go to sleep after the clock keeps him awake? Circle **one**.

the living room   the kitchen   the library

2) Which **two** things keep Mr Bear awake in the kitchen?

a. _____

b. _____

3) Draw lines to match each animal to the noise it makes.

owl	MIAAAOW
hedgehog	TOO-WHIT-TOO-WHOO
cat	SNUFFLE, SNUFFLE

4) Where in the garden were the cats singing?

on the wall ☐

on the fence ☐

on the bench ☐

5) Find and copy **two** words that tell us what it was like in the car.

a. _____

b. _____

6 What happened when Mr Bear started to fall asleep in the car? Tick **two**.

He snored and snored. ☐

The birds started to sing. ☐

The sun peeped in at the window. ☐

7 *"Peace at last," he said to himself.*

Why do you think Mr Bear said this?

_____

_____

_____

8 What did Mr Bear do that shows that he was still tired the next morning?

_____

Punctuation in Action

BRRRRRRRRRRRRRRRR! went the alarm clock, BRRRRRR!

Why has the author used exclamation marks in this sentence (see page 20 for exclamation marks)? Tick **one**.

to show that Mr Bear was angry ☐

to show that Mrs Bear was noisy ☐

to show that the alarm clock was loud ☐

The Bear and the Piano, by David Litchfield

> *The Bear and the Piano* is a best-selling picture book written and illustrated by David Litchfield. It was published in 2016. It tells the story of a young bear cub who finds an abandoned piano in the forest. He learns to play it and becomes a world-famous pianist.

One day in the forest, a young bear cub found something he'd never seen before.

"What could this strange thing be?" he thought. Shyly, he touched it with his stubby paws.

"PLONK!"

The strange thing made an awful sound. So, the bear left. But the next day he came back, and the day after that too. And for days and weeks and months and years, until eventually …

The sounds that came from the strange thing were beautiful, and the bear had grown big and strong and grizzly. When he played, he felt so happy. The sound took him away from the forest, and he dreamed of strange and wonderful lands.

It wasn't long before the other bears in the forest were drawn to the clearing. Every night, a crowd gathered to listen to the magical melodies coming from the bear and the strange thing.

Then, one night, a girl and her father came across the clearing. They told the bear that the strange thing was a piano and the sounds it made were music.

"Come to the city with us," they said. "There is lots of music there. You can play grand pianos in front of hundreds of people and hear sounds so beautiful they will make your fur stand on end."

The bear knew that if he left the forest, the other bears would miss him very much.

But he longed to explore the world beyond the woods, to hear more wonderful music and play better than ever before.

And before long ...

The bear's name was up in big, bright lights in the big, bright city. He played sold-out concerts in giant theatres. Every night, he performed with such passion and such grace, to wild applause and standing ovations and huge admiration.

The bear recorded albums that went platinum. He was interviewed for magazines. He won awards. He met new people every day and created headlines everywhere he went.

The city was everything he had hoped it would be.

The Bear and the Piano, by David Litchfield

1 Where did the bear live when he was a young cub? Tick **one**.

a beach ☐

a forest ☐

a palace ☐

a city ☐

2 *So, the bear left.*

Why did the bear leave? Tick **one**.

Because the strange thing made an awful sound. ☐

Because he didn't know what the strange thing was. ☐

Because he wanted to go for a walk. ☐

Because he was hungry. ☐

3 What did the bear dream of? Circle **one**.

lots of money   pots of honey

strange and wonderful lands   the forest

4 Over time, the sound that the bear made changed. Circle **one** answer to show how the sound changed.

awful to beautiful   beautiful to awful

sad to happy   quiet to noisy

5 Who told the bear that the strange thing was called a piano?

_____

6 Why was the bear worried about leaving the forest?

_____

_____

7 Why did the bear want to leave the forest? Give **one** reason.

_____

_____

8 Do you think the bear was happy in the city?

Yes ☐   No ☐

Give **one** reason for your answer using evidence from the text.

_____

_____

_____

Spelling in Action

"Come to the city with us," they said.

Underline the word in the sentence above that uses the hard 'c' and circle the word that uses the soft 'c' (see page 32 for hard and soft 'c').

How are stars made?

'How are stars made?' is from *My First Question and Answer Book*, which covers key topics in science, history and nature. This extract explains what stars are made from, how long they exist for, where you can find them and lots of other exciting facts!

How are stars made?

Stars are made from huge clouds of dust and gas. Gradually the cloud shrinks and all the gas and dust clump together. The centre of the cloud gets hotter and hotter and a new star begins to shine. The star gives off heat and light.

Shine on!

Stars can shine for thousands and millions of years! The Sun started shining five thousand million years ago. It will stop shining in another five thousand million years.

What is a group of stars called?

A group of stars is called a cluster. A star cluster is made from a giant cloud of gas and dust. Some clusters contain just a few stars. Others contain hundreds of stars and they look like a big ball of light.

Are all stars white?

Only the most giant stars shine with a bright white light. This is because they are extremely hot. Smaller stars, such as our Sun, are not so hot. They look yellow instead. Very small stars are cooler still. They look red or brown.

What is the Milky Way?

The stars in space are in huge groups called galaxies. Our galaxy is called the Milky Way. All the stars in the night sky are in the Milky Way. There are so many that you couldn't count them all in your whole lifetime!

How are stars made?

1) What are stars made from? Circle **one**.

dust and gas   sparkles and glitter   rocks and stones

2) *Gradually the cloud shrinks and all the gas and dust clump together.*

Find and copy the word in this sentence that means the same as 'gets smaller'.

_____

3) Which two things does a star give off? Tick **two**.

heat ☐   shadows ☐

light ☐   sound ☐

4) How many years can stars shine for? Circle **one**.

one thousand   five million   thousands and millions

5) What is the part of the text with the heading **Shine on!** about? Tick **one**.

how shiny stars are ☐   how pretty stars are ☐

how exciting stars are ☐   how long stars shine for ☐

6) What is a group of stars called?

_____

7 Draw lines to match each type of star to the colour it gives off when it shines.

giant star		bright white
Sun		red or brown
small star		yellow

8 Is it possible to count all of the stars in the night sky? Tick **one**.

Yes ☐   No ☐

Explain your answer.

_____

_____

Punctuation in Action

How are stars made?

Which punctuation mark is used in the sentence above (see page 14 for full stops, page 18 for question marks and page 20 for exclamation marks)? Tick **one**.

full stop ☐

question mark ☐

exclamation mark ☐

Your Heart and Lungs, by Sally Hewitt

Your Heart and Lungs is an introduction to how the human body works. This extract explains how amazing the heart is, what it does and how it works.

Your amazing heart

Your heart is a muscle that pumps your blood around your body.

Your heart sits just to the left of the middle of your chest. It is about the size of your fist.

Heart shapes are everywhere – on balloons, cards and cuddly toys. But your real heart looks quite different.

A doctor listens to your heart pumping in your chest using a stethoscope.

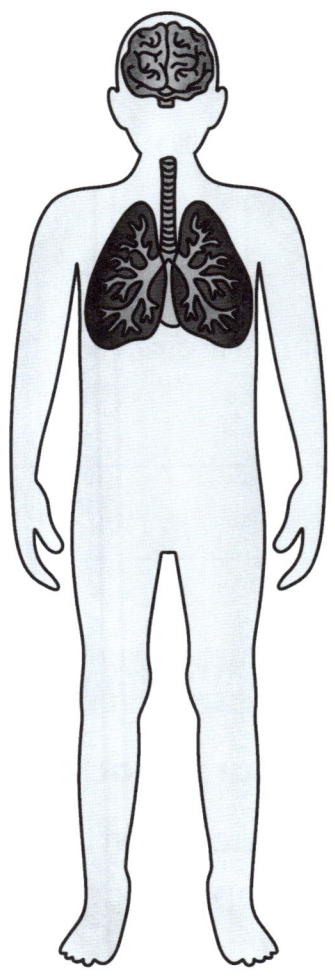

Your heart is always working. It pumps blood all day and all night to all the different parts of your body. Every part of your body – your brain, lungs, skin, etc. – needs blood to keep it working properly.

Your heart doesn't need to work as hard when you are asleep. It has to beat faster when you wake up and start moving.

Heart beat

Your heart muscle squeezes over and over again giving a heart 'beat'.

When your heart fills up with blood, the heart muscle squeezes to push this blood out into your blood vessels. Your heart then fills up with more blood.

Each side of your heart has two rooms or 'chambers'. The right side of your heart pumps blood into your lungs to collect oxygen. The left side pumps this blood back into your body.

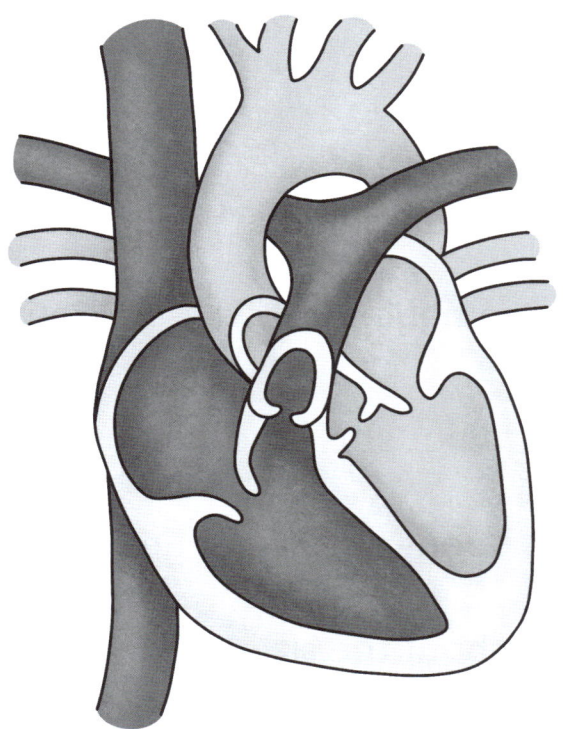

Activity

When you're next in the bath, try filling a rubber duck, squeezy bath toy or even a plastic bottle with water, then squeezing it out. Do it again ... and again! This is like your heart muscles squeezing as it pumps blood.

Be careful where you squirt the water!

Your Heart and Lungs, by Sally Hewitt

1 What does your heart pump around your body? Circle **one**.

  balloons   air   blood

2 Where in your body would you find your heart? Circle **one**.

  in your chest   in your hand   in a cuddly toy

3 What size is your heart? Tick **one**.

  about the size of your fist ☐

  about the size of your head ☐

  about the size of an elephant ☐

  about the size of a balloon ☐

4 Which piece of equipment does a doctor use to listen to your heart?

  _____

5 Tick the sentences that are true.

  Your heart only works at night. ☐

  Your brain needs blood to keep it working. ☐

  Your heart works harder when you are awake. ☐

  Your heart works harder when you are asleep. ☐

6 Draw lines to match the part of the heart to the job that it does.

The left side of your heart	collect oxygen.
The right side of your heart	pumps blood back into your body.
Your lungs	pumps blood into your lungs.

7 Write **one** of the items that you could use to try out the activity.

_____

8 Why do you think the author has suggested doing this activity?

_____

_____

_____

Spelling in Action

A doctor listens to your heart pumping in your chest using a stethoscope.

Your heart is always working. It pumps blood all day and all night to all the different parts of your body.

Find and copy **two** words that end with the suffix –ing from the lines above (see page 38 for the suffix –ing).

a. _____

b. _____

Silver, by Walter de la Mare

'Silver', by the British author and poet Walter de la Mare, is a classic poem that was first published in 1913. The poem describes the moon as a person walking through the night, bathing objects and creatures in her beautiful silver glow.

Slowly, silently, now the moon
Walks the night in her silver shoon;
This way, and that, she peers, and sees
Silver fruit upon silver trees;
One by one the casements catch
Her beams beneath the silvery thatch;
Couched in his kennel, like a log,
With paws of silver sleeps the dog;
From their shadowy cote the white breasts peep
Of doves in a silver-feathered sleep;
A harvest mouse goes scampering by,
With silver claws and a silver eye;
And moveless fish in the water gleam,
By silver reeds in a silver stream.

Silver, by Walter de la Mare

1 Which pair of words best describes how the moon walks? Circle **one**.

fast and loud   slowly and silently   quickly and rushed

2 What colour is the fruit on the trees?

_____

3 Why does the dog have silver paws?

_____

_____

4 Name **three** animals that are mentioned in the poem.

a. _____

b. _____

c. _____

5 Find and copy **two** words that rhyme.

a. _____

b. _____

Spelling in Action

One by one the casements catch
Her beams beneath the silvery thatch

Read these lines from the poem. Underline the **two** words that have the /ch/ sound (see page 28 for 'ch' and 'tch').

Say How You Feel, by Joseph Coelho

'Say How You Feel' is from a modern book of poems called *Poems Aloud*. The aim of the collection is to bring poetry alive by reading it aloud. This poem is written by the award-winning poet and author Joseph Coelho. It is a lively poem about the different emotions that we feel.

When I'm sad
it feels like the sky is crashing down,
like the oceans are rising
and the ground is swallowing me up.
All is dark and cold.

When I'm nervous
it feels like my heart
is going to lightning-strike out of my
chest, like my skin is raining,
like my belly is a mudslide.

When I'm happy
my cheeks feel like rose buds,
my tummy glows with sunlight.
my shoulders are a forest breeze.

When I'm angry
my body is rock,
my face is wet clay.
Meteorites inhabit my fists,
my voice is all smoke and fire.

When I'm excited
my toes are ants,
I'm a river bubbling
and an air current of wishes,
my smile could explode the sun.

Say How You Feel, by Joseph Coelho

1. Which word describes the sky in the first verse? Circle **one**.

   floating   rising   crashing

2. Which **four** parts of the body does the poem mention in the second verse? One has been done for you.

   a. _____heart_____

   b. _____

   c. _____

   d. _____

3. Look at the third verse. What does the narrator of the poem say their cheeks are like?

   _____

4. Look at the fourth verse. What do you think is happening to the narrator's body when he is angry? Explain your answer using evidence from the text.

   _____

   _____

5. How does the narrator of the poem say that they speak when they are angry?

   _____

6 Look at the fifth verse. What does the narrator compare their toes to? Tick **one**.

river ☐

mudslide ☐

forest ☐

ants ☐

7 *my smile could explode the sun*

Why do you think the narrator's smile could explode the sun?

_____

_____

8 What is the poem about? Tick **one**.

the weather ☐

feelings ☐

meteorites ☐

Vocabulary in Action

my tummy glows with sunlight.

'sunlight' is a compound word (see page 46 for compound words). Write the **two** words it is made from.

_____ + _____

Writing skills: What can you see at night?

The 'Writing skills' task is inspired by the themes in the reading comprehension texts. It provides an opportunity to apply the skills practised in this book. Answer guidance can be downloaded from the **Schofield & Sims** website.

1 Use the picture to complete these sentences.

a. I can see a _____ walking along a _____.

b. The _____ can tip the _____.

c. The _____ are in the sky.

2 Write **seven** words about night-time. Use your own ideas, then use the picture in **Question 1**. One has been done for you.

moon

3 Write some sentences about what you can see at night. Think about things you have seen at night in the past and imagine what you might see.

You could:

- Split words into sounds to spell them (page 22)
- Use 'and' to join words together (page 8)
- Use full stops at the end of sentences (page 14).

Re-read 'Peace at Last' (page 60) for some more ideas of what you can see at night.

_____
_____
_____
_____
_____
_____
_____
_____
_____

Tip Check that you have used full stops and capital letters and correct any spelling mistakes.

Final practice

The 'Final practice' includes grammar, punctuation, spelling, vocabulary and reading comprehension questions. Work through the questions carefully and try to answer each one. The target time for completing these questions is 45 minutes. The answers can be downloaded from the **Schofield & Sims** website.

1) Add –s or –es to each word to make it plural.

pear_____ book_____ torch_____

1 mark

2) Write these words in the correct order to make a sentence.

a. are We team. a

_____

b. Are there? nearly we

_____

1 mark

3) Tick any sentences below that use both capital letters and full stops correctly.

Sandra went to London. ☐   luca loves dinosaurs ☐

1 mark

4) Finish this sentence by writing 'and' and your own ending.

I like to go to the park _____

_____

1 mark

5) Write a question mark '?' or an exclamation mark '!' to show how each sentence should end.

a. Help____   **b.** How much is that____

1 mark

Final practice

6 Write the correct word from the box to complete the sentences.

> said   house

a. Sam came to play at my _____.

b. Mr Li _____ we need to bring a coat.

1 mark

7 Write 'f' or 'ph' to complete these words.

a. _____eet

b. _____one

c. dol_____in

d. lea_____

1 mark

8 Unscramble these words to make words that have the hard 'c'.

a. keac _____

b. owlnc _____

1 mark

9 Write the correct word from the box to complete the sentences.

> cross   cliff   fell   fizz

a. My sister _____ and hurt her leg.

b. We climbed a steep _____.

c. The firework went _____!

d. Dad was _____ when his bus was late.

1 mark

10 Write the days of the week in the correct order.

_____

_____

_____

1 mark

Final practice

11 Add –er to each of the words in the box. Use the new words to complete the sentences.

> tall   grand   quick   slow

a. A tortoise is _____ than a cheetah.

b. A giraffe is _____ than a mouse.

c. Driving is _____ than walking.

d. A castle is _____ than a house.

1 mark

12 Draw lines to join the words to make compound words.

ear		stick
rain		phone
gold		bow
drum		fish

1 mark

13 Read the story. Circle the correct word to complete the sentences.

> Once upon a time there were three billy goats. They wanted to eat the fresh, green grass on the other side of the field. To get to the grass they had to cross a bridge.

a. The three goats wanted to eat the **pizza / grass / flowers**.

b. The three goats needed to cross a **bridge / road / hill**.

1 mark

Final practice

14) Look at the list below and answer the questions.

The Green family's shopping list
~~12~~ 6 eggs
strawberry jam
cat food
birthday card for Gran

a. How many eggs do the family need to buy? _____

b. What flavour jam is on the list? _____

c. Who is the birthday card for? _____

1 mark

15) Read the information text below, then tick the box to show whether each sentence is true or false.

Aeroplanes are great for long journeys. They can carry lots of people and they can fly all around the world.

Statement	True	False
Aeroplanes can be good for long journeys.		
Aeroplanes do not carry many people.		

1 mark

16) Read the text. Put the pictures in the correct order by writing the numbers 1, 2, 3 and 4 next to them.

There is one egg on the leaf. The egg hatches and a caterpillar comes out. The caterpillar turns into a cocoon. Then it turns into a beautiful butterfly.

____   ____   ____   ____

1 mark

Primary Practice **English Year 1**

Final practice

17 *People go on a tour called a safari to see animals in the wild.*

What does the word 'tour' mean? Tick **one**.

a race ☐   a shop ☐   a trip ☐

1 mark

18 Read the sentences below. Tick the sentence that must be true based on the first sentence you read.

Jellyfish have a mouth but no brains or eyes.

Jellyfish can see things from a long distance. ☐

Jellyfish cannot see like we can. ☐

1 mark

19 Read these sentences and answer the questions.

> Shen smiled as she skipped to school. She took her snack out of her bag. Mum had packed a banana. Shen pulled a face.

a. Do you think Shen was happy to go to school? Tick **one**.

Yes ☐   No ☐

How do you know? Write **one** reason.

_____

1 mark

b. Find and copy **three** words that show Shen was not happy with her snack.

_____

1 mark

Total:

20 marks